Ball Python Care

The Complete Guide to Caring for and Keeping Ball Pythons as Pets

Pet Care Professionals

ISBN 13: 978-1530251841

CONTENTS

INTRODUCTION

The Ball Python (scientifically named *Python Regius*) is a species that originates from sub-Saharan Africa. The name is based upon the fact that the animal has a tendency to curl itself into a ball when under attack, stressed or frightened. The species is also commonly known as the Royal Python. The name Royal Python anecdotally comes from the fact that African royalty would wear Ball Pythons around their necks as a form of living jewelry. Like other pythons, the Ball Python is a non-venomous constrictor. Ball Pythons are common house hold pets due to their relatively small size, docile temperament and the fact that they are non-venomous.

DESCRIPTION

Ball Pythons are large bodied snakes. They come in a wide variety of colours and morphs (genetic mutations). However, the snakes colorings tend to be more earthy: browns, beiges, or black with gold and white markings. The snakes bellies are usually white or cream and may contain black markings. The snakes body is normally stocky with the head being relatively small in comparison. The scales of the Ball Python are smooth.

Size

Males normally range between 3-3.5ft. Females tend to be larger than males. Females normally range between 4-4.5ft However adult Ball Pythons have been known to grow to be as large as 6ft.

Differences between the sexes

Both sexes have anal spurs on either side of their vent. Males tend to have larger spurs than females despite normally being smaller in overall size. However this is not the best way to determine the sex of the snake. The best way to determine the snakes sex is via manual eversion of the male hemipenes or by inserting a probe into the snakes cloaca. When probing to determine sex it is important to note that females tend to measure 2-4 subcaudal scales and males tend to measure 8-10.

Natural Habitat

Ball Pythons are a terrestrial species which means that they live primarily on the ground. They are likewise mainly nocturnal and inactive during the day. During the day they tend to hide away. They prefer grassland, sparsely wooded areas or savannas. The ideal natural habitats for this species are termite mounds and empty mammal burrows.

Behavior

Being a terrestrial species that is more open to attack, the Ball Python is known for its defensive strategy. It coils into a tight ball when threatened which allows it to hide, and protect, its head and neck in the middle of the ball.

Diet

In the wild, their diet mainly consists of small mammals – mainly rodents such as rats, mice and shrews. However they are also known to consume birds if they are able to get them.

Lifespan

In the wild they generally live for 10 years. However in captivity they more often live between 20-30 years. The oldest recorded Ball Python was an incredible 47 years old!

BALL PYTHONS AS PETS

Ball Pythons are commonly bred in captivity and are popular as pets because of their small size in comparison to other pythons as well as having a docile temperament. They are highly unlikely to bite and will only do so if severely threatened. They are more likely to curl into a protective ball than actually bite. They are easy and safe pets to handle, despite their size, and make good pets for both experienced and beginner snake keepers.

Choosing your Ball Python

I highly recommend always asking to handle the snake before you purchase it. This will allow you to examine the snake for any health or temperament issues before actually parting with money or taking the snake home. A healthy Ball Python will look alert, bright eyed and have a flickering lounge during a handling session. As previously mentioned the scales of the snake should feel smooth and there should be no traces of half shed skin along the snakes body. If you encounter any problems, or have any doubt about the snakes temperament, do not purchase it.

Transporting the Ball Python

Ball Pythons can be easily transported over short distances. Common ways to transport them include plastic tubs with lids or cotton bags which can be tied at the top. Most professional reptile stockiest will provide you with a container to transport the snake but it is worth checking beforehand with both commercial and private sellers.

Handling

As Ball Pythons are a timid species it is common for them to not appreciate being handled for long periods of time. Regular handling is important though to allow your python to get used to human contact. Regular handling is also important to allow the snake to exercise outside of the vivarium. Despite being large in size they are easy to handle due to their tendency to move slowly. Ball Pythons are known to be clumsy snakes which means that you should take care during all handling sessions. A fall from a small height, depending how the snake lands, could critically injure your snake.

Recording

It is highly advisable to keep a record throughout your snakes life. By regularly noting down weight, length, feeding patterns and shedding patterns you will have a useful resource to help notice any potential problems with your python and to likewise make sure it is in good health.

CAN MULTIPLE BALL PYTHONS BE HOUSED TOGETHER?

It is not considered best practice to house multiple Ball Pythons in the same vivarium as there is the potential for multiple problems. However some owners have housed multiple Ball Pythons together without any issues. This section will outline the best practices for housing multiple pythons together to help you make the best choice for your individual case.

Potential Dangers

There are numerous dangers of housing multiple pythons together. If the pythons being housed together are not of a similar age or size there is the potential for cannibalism. There is likewise an increased chance of causing stress in one, or multiple, of the pythons due to the close quarters they are forced to live in. Close quarters also means the spread of disease or illness is far more likely – which would potentially mean that you would have to spend twice as much at the vets! There is also the potential for unexpected breeding to occur so it might be best to house snakes of the same sex to avoid this.

Best Practice when Housing Multiple Ball Pythons

If you decide that you do in fact want to house multiple pythons together it is important to have a large vivarium to accommodate multiple snakes and give them space to be apart from each other. Likewise it is important to have multiple sufficient hiding spots for the snakes as if the hiding spots are not of equal quality the snake that is unable to use them will feel stressed. It is best practice to have a spare vivarium ready in case there are issues and you need to separate your snakes.

SHEDDING

Ball Pythons, like all snakes, periodically shed their outer layer of skin throughout their lives. As a keeper there is nothing to worry about as the shedding process is both natural, painless and important to keep your snake happy and healthy. Young snakes tend to shed their skin more than adult snakes, but generally the shedding process happens several times a year.

Blue Eyes and Dull Skin

If your python's eyes have suddenly turned a bluish grey colour and its skin has become dull do not worry. These changes are called Preecdysis. Preecdysis is the name given to the symptoms which indicate that a python is about to shed its skin. During the shedding process your snake may refuse to eat and not want to be handle. However your snake may have no noticeable change in temperament – it all depends how the individual snake deals with the process of Preecdysis. During Preecdysis it is advisable to handle your snake with care as their vision is impaired due to the blue grey membrane covering their eyes. It is common for pythons to act more defensive during this process.

How can you help?

Some snakes will handle the shedding of their skin easily and not need any assistance but if you want to assist your snake with the shedding process you can raise the humidity in your vivarium: this helps the snake loosen its skin. You can likewise put a bowl of water into the vivarium which will allow the python to soak itself if desired. Another method to help loosen the snake's skin is to mist the inside of the vivarium with water to help further raise the humidity. Even if your snake does not need assistance with the shedding process they will still appreciate the process being made easier for them. However as previously mentioned assisting your snake is, in most cases, not essential.

Ecdysis

Ecdysis is the name given to the actual process of shedding. This process is characterised by your snake rubbing its head on rocks, or material within your vivarium, to loosen the skin around its head. Once it's the skin around its head is loose your python will begin to crawl out of the old skin through a process of rolling the skin inside out as it moves. Once the skin has been fully shed it is best practice to remove it as soon as possible. Shed skin is normally accompanied by excrement.

Unshed Skin

After removing the shed skin from the vivarium it is best to then check your snake for any unshed skin. Pay particular attention to the snakes eye lids and tail as these areas are most common for skin to not fully shed. If there is any skin that has not been shed use a warm towel or tweezers to remove the unshed skin. Removal of the unshed skin will help to avoid infection and damage to the skin tissue bellow it.

FEEDING

In the wild a Ball Python's diet consists of mainly small mammals such as rats, shrews and mice. Ball Pythons are notoriously bad eaters as they will refuse food if they are stressed, not being kept in the correct conditions or do not wish to be handled.

Feeding a Hatchling

It is best practice to feed your hatchling python on small mice. They should be fed once every 5-6 days to encourage their growth. Some owners will feed their pythons twice a week, or feed them two mice instead of one, to encourage weight gain and an increase in length.

Feeding an Adult

Adult pythons should be fed an adult mouse every 7-10 days. This is not as strict however as the amount a python should eat is dependent on its size – for example a larger python may require two adult mice instead of one. Other larger prey can be introduced to create a variation in the python's diet. Variant larger prey normally include: rats, small rabbits and day old chickens.

Live Prey or Frozen?

DO NOT feed your python live prey. Live prey, even a small mouse, can injury your snake. The prey that python's eat normally have sharp teeth or claws and are therefore undesirable as the python may not want to eat them straight away leaving the prey an opportunity to defend themselves. Shop brought frozen mice, and other rodents, are available at most reptile shops and even general pet shops. The frozen prey can also be purchased on the internet. Frozen prey should be thawed to room temperature before used to feed the snake. DO NOT feed your snake wild rodents. Wild rodents carry parasites and may contain suburban toxins that could harm your snake.

How to Feed

Your Ball Python should be fed outside of the vivarium if possible. This eliminates the risk of your snake ingesting any of the substrate used to line your vivarium. If the snake ingests too much substrate it may become unhealthy, ill or may regurgitate its food. It is best to avoid handling your python for about 48 hours after feeding as they are likely to regurgitate their meal.

Braining a Mouse

If your python seems reluctant to eat, 'braining' a mouse is a good way to encourage feeding. Snakes are attracted to the scent of brain matter. If you cut, or use a needle to poke a hole, into the skull of a mouse to expose its brain tissue it will increase the chance of the python feeding.

Bad Eaters

As previously mentioned Ball Pythons are notoriously bad eaters. You should not be concerned if your snake misses a meal every now and then. Instead of trying to force your snake to eat you should focus on making the snake more comfortable: handle it less, make sure the hides within the vivarium are sufficient and make sure the temperature is correct. Once the snake is anxiety free it should resume eating again. Ball Pythons also, normally, do not eat if they are preparing to shed their skin. As previously mentioned it is good to keep a record of your snake's weight, length and feeding habits. By keeping a record you can check if your snake is acting abnormally or in a way that is concerning and take it to a vet.

HOUSING

As Ball Pythons are not highly active there is no need for a large enclosure. Snakes are prone to escape their vivarium's if they are no sealed properly so you must take care when planning their housing. Make sure your vivarium has a tightly fitting lid as Ball Pythons are strong enough to move loosely fitted lids. If your lid does not fit tightly and you are worried about your snake escaping it is advisable to place something, light enough to not damage the lid but heavy enough, to stop the snake escaping on each corner – a good example of this would be thin hardback books.

The Perfect Size Vivarium

The way to work out the perfect size vivarium is to take the length of your snake and make it equal to the front and one of the sides of the vivarium.

Examples:

A 5ft Ball Python would be perfect for a 3ft by 2ft vivarium.

A 3ft Ball Python would be perfect for a 2ft by 1ft vivarium.

The Dangers of an Overly Large Vivarium

If a vivarium is too large, or does not contain enough hiding spots, a Ball Python is likely to feel stressed as they will feel unsafe. This stress may lead the python to stop eating and become underweight which in turn will cause health problems.

Hiding Spots

By nature all Ball Pythons want a place to hide and feel secure and will become stressed if this is not provided for them within their vivarium. Hides can range from cardboard boxes to specially designed ones bought from pet shops. It does not matter what the hide looks like as long as it is big enough to allow the python to curl up inside it while also not being too big as this will not make the python feel secure. It is advisable to have multiple hides in your vivarium and to space them out along the temperature line. This allows for the python to rotate between hides to help control its body temperature.

A Place to Climb

Pythons will climb anything you put into their vivarium. Most people provide their snakes with branches and plastic plants. Branches that have come from outside will have to be debugged and soaked in a chlorine/water solution before being introduced to the vivarium to avoided contamination which could lead to illness and disease. If in doubt about a product/branch DO NOT introduced it to your vivarium.

Mix It Up

Ball Pythons are highly intelligent and inquisitive creatures. It is therefore advisable to change the layout of your vivarium every now and then. Upon reintroducing your python to the newly furnished vivarium you will notice the snake exploring its new surroundings.

Water Bowl

Ball Pythons need fresh water to drink on a daily basis. Water should be provided in a shallow and heavy bowl – to avoid the snake tipping it over. Water bowls must be changed immediately if you notice that the python has defecated in it. Water bowls as previously mentioned can also help during the shedding process.

CONTENTS OF A VIVARIUM

Aspen Shavings

Aspen shavings are great for lining the floor of your vivarium. A great bonus is that they collect urine and faeces and can easily be scooped out with a dog or cat litter scoop. However Aspen shavings have two flaws. Firstly they have to be replaced once they become dirty. Secondly your Python will need to be removed to be fed as they may ingest the shavings by mistake

Note: DO NOT use Cedar or Redwood shavings as they are toxic to snakes.

Beech Chippings

Beech chippings are cheap and readily available from all reptile stores. They are not as absorbent as Aspen shavings and likewise need to be removed once they are dirtied. However they come in three different grades – small, medium and large. This allows you to choose which grade best suits your snake.

Newspaper and Paper Towels

Both newspaper and paper towels are easily obtained and inexpensive. They make for good flooring if your snake has a belly injury as they are smooth and do not have any potentially harmful edges. However there is the potential for harmful inks to be present within the paper which make them not ideal for long term use.

Artificial Grass

There are many grades of artificial grass which allows you to choose which best suits your snakes needs. Artificial grass is widely available in hardware stores and ironically the cheapest is normally the best when it comes to lining a vivarium. The cheapest artificial grass tends to be the most flexible which makes it easier to clean and also less likely to harm your snake's belly. If artificial grass is used it is best practice to have multiple pieces cut to fit the floor of the vivarium. This allows for you to rotate the flooring when needed to clean and dry the other pieces.

HEATING EQUIPMENT

Ball Pythons are cold blooded and therefore rely on their surroundings to get heat. In the wild snakes bask in the sun to keep warm and stay cool by either moving to shady spots of going underground in a mammal burrow or termite hole.

Ceramic Heater

Heat should be provided through a ceramic heater with a pulse thermostat and bulb guard. Ceramic heaters create a good air temperature which is preferred by the Ball Python. Ceramic heaters also tend to create ambient lighting which is again preferred by the snake. Ceramic heaters should be set up on one side of your vivarium to allow your python to thermo-regulate. A ceramic bulb can be purchased from any reptile shop. The wattage of the ceramic bulb needed is dependent on the size of the vivarium you are trying to heat – it is best to ask the clerk at the reptile shop for advice on this to tailor the bulb to your specific vivarium.

Using a Lightbulb as a Heater

It is common for people to also use regular light bulbs to supply heat to their snake's vivarium. However they are not as efficient as they require always being turned on. Ball Pythons do not need 24 hours of light and a constantly lit lightbulb could cause anxiety for the snake. It is therefore advisable to invent in a ceramic heater if you are serious about caring for your snake as they do not cause any form of light-stress.

Bulb Guard

It is vital to have a bulb guard attached to your heater. Snakes do not feel heat in the same way as humans and may not actually realise if they are being burnt by what they are touching. A bulb guard will ensure that your python will stay a safe distance away from the potentially burning bulb.

DISEASE AND ILLNESS

In order to properly care for you snake it is important to be highly observant for signs and symptoms of illness. Often symptoms are not apparent until well into the course of the illness and it is therefore important to promptly address any signs of illness that you notice. Ball Pythons are overall hardy animals and they do not have any unique species specific problems. If you have any concerns about your pets health it is best to seek advice from a veterinarian. Below are some common symptoms to look out for.

Stretching and 'Star Gazing'

If you notice that your snake is lying stretched out or has its head raised (commonly termed 'Star Gazing') for a prolonged period of time it could suggest a respiratory infection and its strange posture could indicate that it is uncomfortable. Serious health concerns, such as paramyxovirus and neurological diseases, can be indicated by 'Star Gazing.'

Soaking

Ball Pythons are not known for spending a lot of time in water except for when they are trying to help along the shedding process. If your snake is spending an excessive amount of time in its water dish it could indicate that it has mites or that it is having problems thermo-regulating.

Breathing Difficulties

Prolonged stress or exposure to pathogens can cause

respiratory illnesses in Ball Pythons. Respiratory infections can cause wheezing, labored breathing or mucus to be produced out the snakes nose. Respiratory problems can be easily fixed if they are caught early but can likewise quickly turn lethal if left uncheck.

Skin Problems

Minor skin injuries will heal themselves within a shed or two and therefore require no special treatment. Major injuries should be treated with veterinary care. Ball Pythons can develop sepsis. Sepsis is characterised by blisters filled with clear fluid and should be immediately treated with veterinary care as it is a serious malady. Sepsis can be avoided by having good, dry and warm conditions within the vivarium.

Anorexia

As previously mentioned Ball Pythons are notoriously difficult feeders. There are a plethora of mundane reasons as to why a Ball Python may refuse a meal. However refusal of a meal could suggest that the snake has parasites or an infection. If you become worried about your snake's refusal of food, or if it loses a significant amount of weight, seek veterinary care.

Lumps

Lumps under the skin can mean multiple different things, none of which can be diagnosed without the specialist knowledge of a veterinarian. If your snake has recently eaten any abnormal lumps may be due to the digestion of the meal as it moves through the snake's system. However lumps can also indicate broken bones, abscesses, tumors or parasites. If the lumps are not associated with feeding seek veterinary care.

Activity Patterns

Many new owners are concerned by their snakes lack of movement within the day light hours. Pythons are mainly nocturnal and in the wild spend the day in mammal burrows or termite mounds. Therefore there is no reason to worry if your snake spends most of the day curled up or hidden within one of the hides within the vivarium.

FINAL THOUGHTS

Thank you for purchasing our pet care manual on the African Ball Python. We hope you have found the information both interesting and informative. We hope that this book has allowed you to make an informed choice on whether owning a Ball Python suits you and if so we hope that the information will help you to provide the best quality care for your pet python.

We will be publishing multiple other pet care manuals on our author page on Kindle. If you have an interest in exotic and exciting pets then we highly suggest you check out our other work.

Here at Pet Care Professionals we are passionate about providing the best quality information to our customers. We would highly appreciate any feedback, or reviews, you could leave us on our Kindle page to allow us to help create the best possible pet care products available on the market.

ABOUT THE AUTHOR

Here at Pet Care Professionals we are passionate about pet care. As a brand we have a strong idea of what makes up a good pet care book. We consult with multiple experts in each animals field to allow us to create a book filled with cumulative opinions and best practices. The experts we consult range from veterinarians to every day pet keepers who have had years of experience caring for the specific animal each book is on. Our aim, and mission, is to produce the best possible pet care books that are a great value for money.

CPSIA information can be obtained at www.ICGtesting.com
Printed in the USA
LVOW10s1856240716

497581LV00043B/1843/P